10 Propositions Regarding Air Power

Colonel Phillip S. Meilinger, USAF
School of Advanced Airpower Studies

I0152881

Air Force History and Museums Program
1995

Author's Note

This work is the product of many minds and ideas, but I would like especially to thank my faculty and student colleagues in the School of Advanced Airpower Studies, as well as the following who have been particularly helpful: Dr. I. B. Holley, Jr., Col. John Roe, Drs. Don LeVine and Dan Kuehl, Lt. Cols. Ernie Howard, Jason Barlow and Tim Gann, Maj. John Farquhar, Drs. Dave Mets and Hal Winton, and Group Captain Gary Waters (RAAF).

Foreword

Though we are still within the first century of powered flight, air power has already become the dominant form of military power projection in the modern world. The doctrinal underpinnings of air power thought are, of course, traditionally ascribed to the three great theorists of air power application, Douhet, Trenchard, and Mitchell. Since the Second World War, the air power community has not often explored the doctrinal implications of air power development. Lord Tedder's Lee Knowles lectures at Cambridge, and the writings of Air Vice Marshal R. A. Mason, and Colonel John A. Warden III constitute notable—and noteworthy—exceptions. Now comes Colonel Phillip Meilinger, who has posited a group of provocative propositions that will instill an appreciation for air power for those who seek to understand it and challenge the assumptions of those who do not yet appreciate what it offers. This book has been deliberately designed in a small format so that it can be readily carried in the pocket of a flight suit or a BDU. Readers are encouraged to discuss these propositions and, if so moved, to communicate directly with Colonel Meilinger via the School of Advanced Airpower Studies, Maxwell AFB, Alabama, or through the Office of the Air Force Historian, Bolling AFB, Washington, D.C.

Richard P. Hallion
Air Force Historian
February 1995

Ten Propositions Regarding Air Power

1. Whoever controls the air generally controls the surface.

2. Air Power is an inherently strategic force.

3. Air Power is primarily an offensive weapon.

4. In essence, Air Power is targeting, targeting is intelligence, and intelligence is analyzing the effects of air operations.

5. Air Power produces physical and psychological shock by dominating the fourth dimension—time.

6. Air Power can conduct parallel operations at all levels of war, simultaneously.

7. Precision air weapons have redefined the meaning of mass.

8. Air Power's unique characteristics necessitate that it be centrally controlled by airmen.

9. Technology and air power are integrally and synergistically related.

10. Air Power includes not only military assets, but an aerospace industry and commercial aviation.

1 ———————➤

Whoever controls the air generally controls the surface.

If we lose the war in the air we lose the war and we lose it quickly.
—Field Marshal Bernard Montgomery

Some refer to this concept as command of the air, others as air superiority, but the point is clear: the first mission of an air force is to defeat or neutralize the enemy air force so friendly operations on land, sea and in the air can proceed unhindered, while at the same time one's own vital centers and military forces remain safe from air attack. Virtually all air theorists subscribe to this proposition. Douhet, for example, stated simply: "to have command of the air is to have victory."[1] In a similar vein, John Warden wrote: "Since the

German attack on Poland in 1939, no country has won a war in the face of enemy air superiority. . . Conversely, no state has lost a war while it maintained air superiority."[2] Whether such a statement is true in unconventional warfare is debatable; but the armies of Germany, Japan, Egypt and Iraq would certainly agree that conventional ground operations are difficult if not impossible when the enemy controls the air.

This emphasis on gaining air superiority often troubles ground commanders who tend to equate proximity with security. Rather than have aircraft attack airfields or aircraft factories in the quest for air superiority, they prefer to have them close by and on call in the event enemy planes appear. This is an understandable desire, but a misguided one, because it would be unwise to tether air power to a static, defensive role. An aggressive doctrine has been very effective for the United States: American troops have not had to fight without air superiority since 1942; the last American ground soldier killed by air attack was in 1953; and our army has never had to fire a surface-to-air missile at an enemy aircraft—they have never been allowed to get that close.[3] In actuality, our Army's doctrine assumes friendly air superiority, and sees its achievement as one of air power's biggest contributions to land operations.

This need for air cover also extends to maritime operations. As early as the First World War naval aviators like John Towers saw the need for aircraft carriers to ensure air superiority over the fleet. For many years this view was not accepted by surface admirals, but Pearl Harbor and the sinking of the British capital ships *Prince of Wales* and *Repulse* by Japanese land-based aircraft in 1941 soon made it clear that ships required air cover to operate effectively. Aircraft carriers provided the mobile air bases for the planes that would help to ensure air superiority over the fleet, while at the same time increasing the ability to project power ashore.[4] The armadas that conquered the central Pacific in World War II were based on aircraft carriers, not battleships, and this emphasis has been reflected in the U.S. Navy's force structure ever since.

The clear implication in the writings of the air theorists is that gaining air superiority is so important it might bring victory: air superiority could be an end in itself. There are two problems with this construct. First, air superiority is only valuable if the political will is available to exploit it. United Nations aircraft can easily dominate the skies over Bosnia or Somalia, for example, but how can that air superiority be exploited? If intransigent opponents do not believe air strikes against their industry or military forces will follow, then control of the air becomes meaningless. Second, it re-introduces the concept of the decisive counter-force battle. Just as an army that invades another country and deliberately bypasses the enemy army while marching on the interior risks the occupation of its own country or the severing of its supply lines, so too an air force that goes straight for the heart of a nation while ignoring the enemy air force courts catastrophe. Consequently, if the fate of nations hinges on the campaign for command of the air, then presumably a belligerent will focus his efforts and resources in that area. If that occurs; the air battle can be just as prolonged, deadly, and subject to the grinding effects of attrition as any land war. This happened in World War II: air power did not eliminate the trench carnage of the Great War; it just moved it to twenty thousand feet. In reality, the attainment of air superiority has not yet brought a country to its knees. Therefore, the proposition remains that air superiority is a necessary but insufficient factor in victory. It is the essential first step.

2 ⟶

Air Power is an inherently strategic force.

Air power has become predominant, both as a deterrent to war, and—in the eventuality of war— as the devastating force to destroy an enemy's potential and fatally undermine his will to wage war.

—General Omar Bradley

War and peace are decided, organized, planned, supplied and commanded at the strategic level of war. Political and military leaders located in major cities direct the efforts of their industry, natural resources and populations to raise and equip military forces. These "vital centers" of a country are generally located well behind the borders and are protected by armies and defensive fortifications. Thus, before the invention of the airplane a nation at war generally hurled its armies against those of an enemy in order to break through to the more vulnerable interior. Some still think this way, as exemplified by a noted military historian who recently wrote: "According to Clausewitz and common sense, an army in wartime succeeds by defeating the enemy army. Destroying the ability of the opponent's uniformed forces to function effectively eliminates what stands in the way of military victory."[5] Sometimes a country was fortunate and was able to annihilate its opponent's army, as Napoleon did at Austerlitz and Jena-Auerstadt, and this could bring quick capitulation. But more often battles were bloody and indecisive; wars were exercises in attrition or exhaustion. As wars became more total, armed forces larger, and societies more industrialized, the dream of decisiveness usually became an unattainable chimera. Armies became tactical implements that ground away at the enemy army, hoping that an accumulation of battlefield victories would position them for decisive, strategic operations.[6]

To an extent, navies are also condemned to fight at the tactical level of war. Once command of the sea has been gained, a fleet can do more: bombard fortresses near shore, enforce a blockade, or conduct amphibious operations. In the first case, however, the results are limited by the range of the ships' guns; in the second the results are felt only indirectly and over time. Certainly a blockade can deprive a belligerent of items needed to sustain the war effort; however, the blockaded party can substitute and redistribute its resources to compensate for what has been denied. In short, indirect economic warfare takes much time, and indeed, there are few instances when a blockade has brought a country to its knees.[7] In the last instance, amphibious operations are generally only a prelude to sustained land operations, but this merely takes us back to the cycle of army versus army.

Air power changed things by compressing the line between the strategic and tactical levels. Aircraft can routinely conduct operations that achieve strategic level effects. To a great extent airplanes obviate the need to confront terrain or the environment because of their ability to fly over armies, fleets and geographic obstacles and strike directly at a country's key centers. This capability offers alternatives to both bloody and prolonged ground battles and deadly naval blockades. In truth, although early air theorists often spoke of the potential of this concept, it was largely a dream for many decades. Air power did not remove the need for a land campaign in Europe during the Second World War, and although an invasion of Japan proper was unnecessary, the evidence was not clear-cut—it took four years and the combined operations of all the services to set the stage for the final and decisive air phase. Korea and Vietnam proved to many that air power was not an effective strategic weapon, although some would maintain it was never given the chance to prove itself.[8] Desert Storm, on the other hand, came close to realizing the claims of the early theorists. Whether it was the fulfillment of prophecy or an aberration remains to be seen.

If the former, then Desert Storm confirms the premise that the goal of the air commander is to maximize his intrinsic advantage by operating at the strategic level of war while forcing the enemy to fight at the tactical level. It is this type of mismatch that coalition air power achieved in the Gulf when, for example, Iraqi air defenses were deprived of centralized control and thus devolved into ineffectual tactical operations, devoid of strategic significance. Although air power can also be employed at the operational and tactical levels, such instances should be considered closely to ensure the effect intended is worth the candle. In essence, air war requires broad, strategic thinking. The air commander must view war in totality, not in a sequential or circumscribed fashion.

Finally, it must be noted that air power has great strategic capabilities as a non-lethal force. In an interesting observation, John Warden noted that, basically, air power delivers strategic information: some of it is "negative" like bombs, and some is "positive" like food. For example, the Berlin Airlift of 1948–49 was perhaps the greatest

Western victory of the Cold War prior to the fall of the Berlin Wall itself. Yet, the Airlift was a demonstration of air power's peaceful application. After the Soviets shut off all land routes into West Berlin, airlifters supplied all the food, medicine, coal and other essentials needed by the population over the next ten months. The result of the Airlift was enormous: the city remained free. This was a strategic victory of the first order, not in the least diminished because it was achieved without firing a shot. The evolving world calls for a greater reliance on airlift, both for force projection and humanitarian assistance. Advances in technology similarly emphasize the importance of space-based air assets such as communications and reconnaissance satellites that ensure nearly instantaneous command and control of military forces, highly accurate location reporting, intelligence gathering and treaty verification. Strategic air power is growing, not decreasing, in importance in our national security structure.

3 ━━━━━━━━━━━━━━━━➤

Air Power is primarily an offensive weapon.

War, once declared, must be waged offensively, aggressively. The enemy must not be fended off, but smitten down.

—Admiral Alfred Thayer Mahan

It is an axiom of surface theorists that the defense is the stronger form of war. By this it is meant that a country or army that is in a weak position will generally assume the defensive because it offers certain advantages. A defender can dig in, build fortifications, and operate on interior lines in friendly, familiar terrain. An attacker therefore has to assault this well prepared enemy, usually by exposing himself to enemy fire. Moreover, the deeper one advances into enemy territory, the farther he is from his sources of supply. These innate strengths led Sun-Tzu to comment: "Being invincible lies with defense; the vulnerability of the enemy comes with the attack."[9] The standard rule was that it took a three-to-one superiority at the point of attack to overcome a foe in prepared positions. As a result, emphasis was placed on assaulting the enemy where he was not expecting it, thus ensuring superior numbers at the crucial point. It must be understood, however, that the same theorists who believe the defense is the stronger form of war also admit that one seldom wins wars by remaining on the defensive; offensive action will eventually be essential. Thus, a defender must husband his resources in preparation for going over to the attack at a favorable opportunity.

Air power does not fit this formulation. The immensity and tracklessness of the sky allows one to strike from any direction; armies generally move over well defined routes. Interception is the key issue here; certainly, radar will be watchful for an air attacker, but terrain masking, electronic measures, careful routing and stealth technology make it extremely difficult to anticipate and prepare for an air assault. H. G. Wells commented in 1908 that there were no highways in the sky; all roads led everywhere. He was, and still is, correct. There are no flanks or fronts in the sky, so an air defender has little chance of channeling an enemy into a predictable path so his defenses can be more effective, or of building fortifications in the sky. It is virtually impossible to stop an air attack completely—some planes will get through. Even when Eighth Air Force bombers suffered "disastrous" losses in strikes against Schweinfurt in 1943, over 85 percent of the bombers penetrated enemy defenses and struck their targets. Surface forces, on the other hand, generally either break through or are repelled—all or nothing.

Moreover, in order to defend all his vital areas, an air defender must spread his squadrons widely, and each point protected must have sufficient strength to drive back an attacker.[10] Unlike on the surface, the air defender has no implicit advantage—passive defense is impractical. Whereas the attacker can strike virtually anything, the defender is limited to striking the attackers. This is inefficient. In addition, an effective defense requires a well organized, responsive and survivable command and control network; the offense does not. Even if such a defensive system is in place, however, dispersion in an attempt to cover all a country's vital areas may grant *de facto* local air superiority to an attacker. In short, in air warfare the defender is stripped of his innate three-to-one superiority, and an air defender theoretically needs more forces than the attacker, the precise opposite of the situation on the ground.[11] This line of reasoning led Douhet and others to term the airplane the offensive weapon *par excellence*. If true, then interesting conclusions follow.

First, a reward is reaped by assuming the offensive. To wait in the air is to risk defeat; therefore, an overwhelming air strike offers great temptation. When such attacks are carried out, they can have devastating effects, as at Pearl Harbor, the Arab-Israeli War of 1967, and Desert Storm. At the very least the need for maintaining the initiative necessitates a sufficient air force-in-being that is ready for immediate and decisive action upon the outbreak of hostilities. In air war there is no time for a mobilization that takes weeks or months; the conflict may be over before it can take effect.

Similarly, Sun-Tzu's dictum that a wise commander defeats his enemy's strategy is inappropriate in air war because it assumes one will wait to see what that strategy is, then move to counteract it. Not only is this a risky business—one can easily be mistaken in guessing the opponent's strategy and therefore counter the wrong move—but it once again surrenders the initiative to the enemy.[12] Finally, the concept of offensive air power obviates the need for a tactical reserve. Land forces establish a reserve whose mission is to stand ready to either exploit success or reinforce a threatened point. Both of these scenarios imply a reactive and defensive posture. Air battles, on the other hand, occur and end so quickly that except in very limited circumstances, air commanders should avoid holding a reserve; instead, they should commit all available aircraft to combat operations.[13] In truth, this issue is ambivalent enough to warrant further study. Clearly, a reserve as meant in land operations is not applicable to air war. But could one argue that aircraft based in a different country hundreds of miles distant yet only minutes away from the battlespace actually constitute a "tactical reserve"?[14]

In summary, the speed, range and flexibility of air power grant it ubiquity, and this in turn imbues it with an offensive capability. Because success in war is generally attained while on the offensive, the adage, "the best defense is a good offense," is almost always true in air war.

4 ⟶

In essence, Air Power is targeting, targeting is intelligence, and intelligence is analyzing the effects of air operations.

How can any man say what he should do himself if he is ignorant what his adversary is about?

—Baron Antoine-Henri Jomini

Air power—both lethal and non-lethal—can be directed against almost anything. The Gulf War showed that digging deeply and using tons of steel and concrete will not guarantee protection from precision penetration bombs. The hardened bunkers of the Iraqi Air Force were designed to withstand a nuclear attack, but they could not survive a perfectly placed high explosive bomb. However, being able to strike anything does not mean one should strike everything. Selecting objectives to strike or influence is the essence of air strategy. Virtually all the air theorists recognized this; unfortunately, they were frustratingly vague on the subject.

Douhet, for example, left it to the genius of the air commander to determine an enemy's "vital centers."[15] He did, however, single out popular will as being of first importance. He predicted that if the people were made to feel the harshness of war—through the bombing of urban areas using high explosives, gas and incendiaries—they would rise up and demand their government make peace. Other theorists had different candidates for which targets should be given priority. The Air Corps Tactical School devised a doctrine concentrating on enemy industry. Their "industrial web" theory characterized a nation's structure as a network of connected and interdependent systems; like a house of cards, if just the right piece was removed the entire edifice would collapse and with it a country's capacity to wage war.[16] The RAF's Jack Slessor emphasized the vulnerability of a country's transportation structure; he advocated the interdiction of troops and supplies as the best method of achieving objectives.[17] John Warden stressed leadership. It was a country's leaders that made decisions regarding peace and war; therefore, all air efforts should be focused on the will of those leaders to induce them to make peace.[18] The early writings of Billy Mitchell (pre-1925) saw the enemy army as the primary target of strategic air power.[19] Thus, all the classic air theorists have had similar notions regarding centers of gravity, but they diverged on singling out the most important one. Indeed, a skeptic could argue that a history of air strategy is a history of the search for the single, perfect target.[20] Nevertheless, this basic framework for determining air strategy was a useful first step—but only a first step.

Air power's ability to affect targets has always exceeded its ability to identify them. The Gulf War demonstrated that if one does not know a target exists, air power may be ineffective. For example, although coalition aircraft destroyed most of the known nuclear, chemical and biological research facilities in Iraq, far more were unknown and not discovered until United Nations inspectors roamed the country after the war.[21] It is an evasion for airmen to claim this was a failure of intelligence not of air power, because the two are integrally intertwined and have always been so. Intelligence is essential to targeting; moreover, intelligence specifically geared to air war is required. Military information-gathering agencies have existed for centuries, but their products were of a tactical nature: how many troops does the enemy possess; where are they located; what is their route of march; what is the rate of fire of their latest weapons? Although such tactical information was also necessary for airmen to fight the tactical air battle, strategic air warfare demanded more; what was the structure of an enemy's society and industry: where were the steel mills and power plants; how did civilian and military leaders communicate with their subordinates; where were the major rail yards; how far advanced was their chemical warfare program; who were the key leaders in society and what were their power bases? These types of questions, essential to an air planner, had seldom been asked before the airplane because they did not need to be.[22] One analyst even argues that intelligence has become "a strategic resource that may prove as valuable and influential in the post-industrial era as capital and labor have been in the industrial age."[23] In this formulation, the key to all conflict is intelligence.

The third step, and no less important than the first two, is analyzing the effects of air attacks. One aspect of this problem is termed bomb damage assessment (BDA), but it is only one aspect, and one with largely tactical implications. The simplest way of determining BDA is through post-attack reconnaissance; however, with the advent of precision munitions this is often inadequate. During the Gulf War, for example, an intelligence headquarters building was struck by coalition aircraft; BDA reported the sortie was 25 percent effective because one-quarter of the building was destroyed. Yet, the wing of the building hit was precisely where the actual target was located, so in reality the sortie was totally effective. The BDA process was using a measurement technique appropriate to the past when precision was unobtainable so obliteration was necessary.[24] In short, BDA is as much an art as a science, and it is often difficult to determine the effects of a precision air strike.

The assessment problem at the strategic level is far more complex. There are at present insufficient standards to measure the effectiveness of strategic airstrikes. In some instances, such as an electrical power network, the relationship between destruction and effectiveness is not linear. For example, during Desert Storm Iraq shut down some of its power plants even though they had not been struck, apparently hoping this would shield them from attack. Because the coalition's intent was to turn off the power not to destroy it, the threat of attack was as effective as the attack itself. Thus, a small number of bombs produced an enormous power loss.[25] Unfortunately, although it can be ascertained that a power plant is not generating electricity, it is far more difficult to judge how that will affect the performance of an air defense network—which may be the true goal of the attack.

This assessment problem has haunted air planners for decades. There are still heated debates as to the effectiveness of strategic bombing during World War II. Were the targets selected the correct ones, or was there a better way to have fought the air war? Surprisingly, this question has not been answered by computer war games, which are unable to assess the strategic effects of air attack. Because of the visual impressiveness of computer war games, however, participants are mistakenly led to believe they are engaged in a scientific exercise. The challenge for airmen is to devise methods of analyzing the relationships between complex systems within a country, determining how best to disrupt them, and then measuring the cascading effect of a system's failure throughout an economy.[26] We are a quantitative society with a need to count and measure things, especially our effectiveness. In the military this tends towards body counts, tonnage figures, sortie rates, percentage of hits on target, etc. Such mechanisms are especially prevalent in air war because there is no clear-cut way of determining progress. Surface forces can trace lines on a map; airmen must count sorties and analyze sometimes obscure and conflicting intelligence data. The real air assessment usually comes after the war. How do we break out of this American penchant for "Nintendo warfare"? Because air power is a strategic force, we must better understand, measure, and predict its effectiveness at that level of war. For too long airmen have relied upon a "faith-based" targeting philosophy that emphasizes logic and common sense rather than empirical evidence.

5 ————————➤

Air Power produces physical and psychological shock by dominating the fourth dimension—time.

How true it is that in all military operations time is everything.

—Duke of Wellington

When discussing the reasons for his success at Austerlitz, Napoleon noted that he, unlike his opponents, understood the value of a minute. He understood the importance of time. In truth, Napoleon was referring more to *timing*. Synchronizing the actions of multiple units so as to maximize their effect is vital; this is timing. It is equally important, however, to think of time as duration. A commander must consider how long it will take to move his units into position, and then to actually employ them. More importantly, he must realize that when force is applied rapidly it has both physical and psychological consequences that dissipate when it is employed gradually. Air power is the most effective manager of time in modern war because of its ability to telescope events. It produces shock.

Although it is difficult to separate the physical and psychological components of shock, the two are decidedly different. Physical shock is produced when force collides with an object. It includes an element of overwhelming power; it is irresistible. Prior to this century shock was generally produced by heavy cavalry, although at times heavily armed infantry deployed in column could also achieve this effect. Indeed, when handled properly, a charge of mounted troops produced enormous shock, sometimes sweeping away the enemy force, as at Arbela and Rossbach. This was not always the case; firepower could at times repel such a cavalry charge, as at Crecy and Waterloo. Nonetheless, shock effect on the battlefield is still important, although today it is generally provided by armored forces. Air power can similarly produce physical shock because of the enormous amount of fire power it can deliver in a concentrated area. The impact of a B–52 loaded with nineteen tons of high explosive bombs is legendary, and even one F–15E can drop four tons of bombs on a spot with a footprint no greater than a good-sized house.

More importantly, air power can produce psychological effects. At its most fundamental level war is psychological. It may be that the best way to increase psychological shock is to increase physical shock, but one must be careful not to equate destruction with effectiveness. Rather, a commander should capitalize on air power's speed and ubiquity—its ability to dramatically increase the tempo of combat operations. The importance of these characteristics can be realized when it is remembered that even the most energetic army is constrained by its speed of march. In studying thousands of campaigns over several centuries, one U.S. Army researcher discovered that mechanized and armored forces stand still between 90 and 99 percent of the time. While heavily engaged with the enemy, they generally advance at the rate of approximately three miles per day, about the same as for infantry. There have been exceptions over the years of course, but the study concludes that rates of ground advance have not appreciably changed over the past four centuries despite the advent of the internal combustion engine and the changes it has brought to the battlefield.[27]

Air power increases speed of movement by orders of magnitude. Aircraft routinely travel several hundred miles into enemy territory at speeds in excess of seven hundred miles per hour. Such mobility means a commander can move so rapidly in so many different directions, regardless of surface obstacles, that a defender is at a severe disadvantage. This conquest of time by air power provides surprise, and surprise in turn affects the mind, causing confusion and disorientation. John Boyd's entire theory of the OODA Loop (observe-orient-decide-act) is based on the premise that telescoping time—arriving at decisions or locations rapidly—is the decisive element in war because of the enormous psychological strain it places on an enemy.[28] In addition, speed and surprise can sometimes substitute for mass: if an enemy is unprepared physically or mentally for an attack, then force, rapidly and unexpectedly applied, can overwhelm him: France in 1940 and Russia in 1941. Moreover, surprise and speed can help reduce casualties because the attackers are less exposed to enemy fire. This is one reason jet aircraft quickly replaced piston-driven aircraft for most tactical air missions in the world's air forces: speed equaled survival.

Nuclear weapons offer the most compelling example of how psychological shock is produced by air power. Man has not increased the destructive power of his weapons in centuries. The Romans destroyed Carthage totally, razing its buildings, killing its inhabitants and sowing its soil with salt so nothing would grow. The destruction at Hiroshima and Nagasaki caused by blast pressure and radiation had similar results. The difference between these instances is that it took several Roman legions over two decades to cause such destruction; it took a single B–29 only two seconds. It was this instantaneous destruction, this conquest of time not of matter, that so impacted the will of the Japanese people and the world in general. And indeed, it still does.

This leads to an important insight regarding the effectiveness of air power in low intensity conflicts. Because guerrilla war is protracted war, by its very nature it is ill-suited for air power, denying it the ability to achieve decision quickly.[29] Campaigns like Rolling Thunder during the Vietnam War indicate that air power is particularly ineffective when denied the opportunity to telescope time. In these instances the limitations of air power are magnified. Indeed, when robbed of its time dimension, the psychological impact of air power may be virtually negative.

6

Air Power can conduct parallel operations at all levels of war, simultaneously.

Whereas to shift the weight of effort on the ground from one point to another takes time, the flexibility inherent in Air Forces permits them without change of base to be switched from one objective to another in the theater of operations.

—Field Marshal Bernard Montgomery

The size of an army is usually determined by the size of the enemy's army (or that of the coalition arrayed against him), because the goal of the commander is to win the counterforce battle. Once that is achieved— and that can take a long time and be quite costly—the army can be used for such things as occupation and administrative duties, but that is not its main purpose, and in any event such tasks can be effectively conducted by police or other paramilitary forces. On the other hand, the size of an air force is not so dependent on the size of the enemy air force because fighting the air battle is only one of the many missions that air power can conduct. More importantly, these other missions, such as strategic attack against centers of gravity, interdiction operations, or close air support of ground troops in combat, are of potentially greater significance and can be conducted contemporaneously with the air superiority campaign.

Parallel operations occur when different campaigns, against different targets, and at different levels of war, are conducted simultaneously. Unlike surface forces that must generally fight sequentially and win the tactical battle before they can move on to operational or strategic objectives, air forces can fight separate campaigns at different levels of war. While carrying out the strategic mission of striking a country's armaments industry, for example, air power is able to conduct an operational level campaign to disrupt an enemy's transportation and supply system. Meanwhile, an air force may also be attacking an opponent's fielded forces at the tactical level. This is precisely what occurred in Desert Storm. While F–117s, F–15s, F–111s and Tornados struck Iraqi nuclear research facilities, oil refineries and airfields, F/A–18s, F–16s and Jaguars bombed rail yards and bridges in southern Iraq to reduce the flow of troops and supplies to the Iraqi army. At the same time A–10s, AV–8s and helicopters flew thousands of sorties against Iraqi troops and equipment in Kuwait. In sum, although one never refers to a tactical and strategic army or navy, one does talk of tactical and strategic air forces. It is of great significance that one can do so, acknowledging air power's flexibility.

Similarly, air power can concurrently conduct different types of air campaigns at the same level of war, such as an air superiority campaign and a strategic bombing campaign. Indeed, it may even be implementing a third or fourth separate strategic campaign as during World War II when at the same time it was bombing German industry and contesting with the Luftwaffe for air superiority over Europe, it was also winning the Battle of the Atlantic against German submarines and choking off the reinforcements to Rommel's troops in North Africa.

Finally, and perhaps most importantly, air power's speed and range allow it to strike targets across the entire depth and breadth of an enemy country. Aircraft do not have to disengage from one battle in order to move to another—an extremely risky and complicated maneuver for land forces. Once having disengaged, aircraft do not have to traverse muddy roads, cross swollen rivers or redirect supply lines in order to fight somewhere else. An excellent example of this was given by the Israeli Air Force in the 1973 Yom Kippur War. The Israelis constantly shifted air power from the Sinai front to the Golan Heights front, from interdiction to close air support, and they were able to make these shifts on a daily basis over a period of several weeks.

Such parallel operations can also have parallel effects, presenting an enemy with multiple crises that occur so quickly he cannot respond effectively to any of them. The most devastating demonstration of this was during the first two days of the Gulf War when hundreds of coalition aircraft hit, among other targets, the Iraqi air defense system, electric power plants, nuclear research facilities, military headquarters, telecommunications towers, command bunkers, intelligence agencies and a presidential palace. These attacks occurred so quickly and so powerfully against several of Iraq's centers of gravity that to a great extent the country was immobilized and the war decided in those first few hours. It was extremely difficult to move troops and supplies, give orders, receive reports from the field, communicate with the people, operate radar sites, or plan and organize an effective defense, much less contemplate an offensive counterattack. Although some questioned the worthiness of Iraq as an opponent, the map on page 39 demonstrates how similar parallel attacks would have looked against Washing-

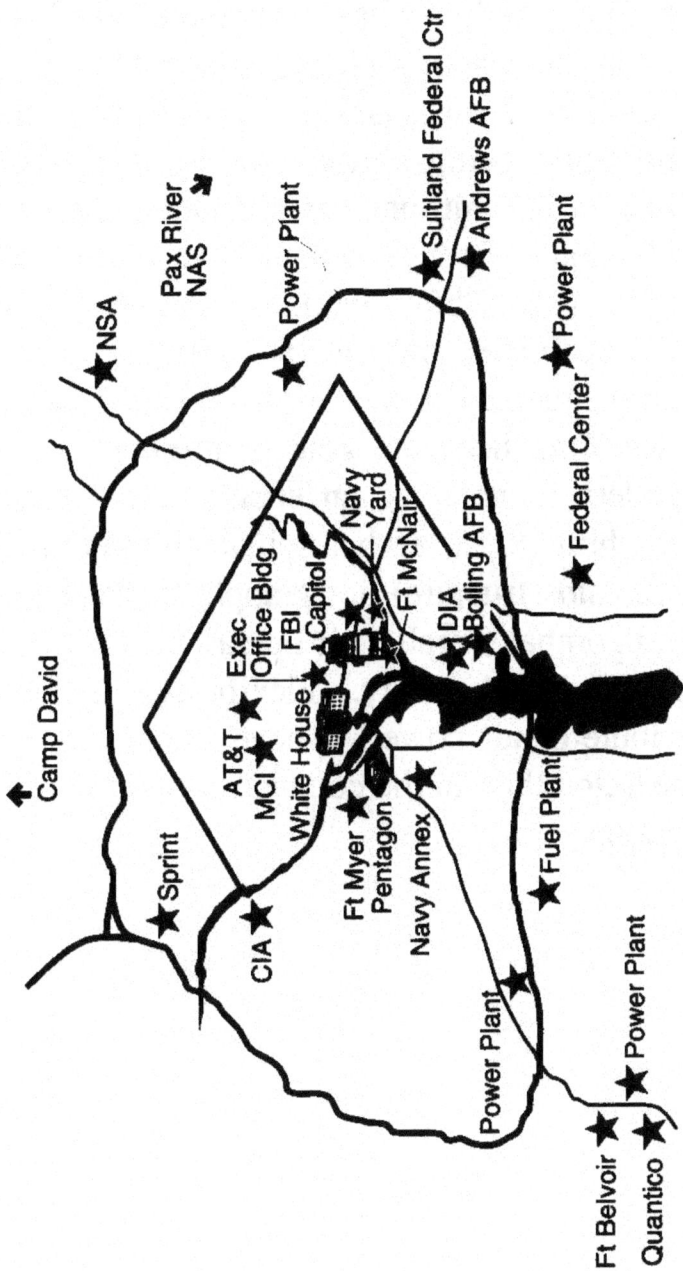

ton, D.C. Could we have maintained our balance in the face of such an onslaught?

Bearing in mind air operations were at the same time being carried out against Iraqi forces in Kuwait, one can appreciate the impact parallel operations can have on an enemy. It is the "brain warfare" envisioned by J. F. C. Fuller, only at the strategic rather than the tactical or operational levels of war. It has long been the goal of military commanders to paralyze an enemy rather than fight him, to sever his spinal column (the command structure) not grapple in hand-to-hand combat. Parallel air operations now offer this opportunity. Flexibility, a key attribute of air power, is never more clearly illustrated than in the conduct of parallel operations.

7

Precision air weapons have redefined the meaning of mass.

Of what use is decisive victory in battle if we bleed to death as a result of it?

—Sir Winston Churchill

Mass has long been considered one of the principles of war. In order to break through an enemy defense, one had to concentrate force and firepower at a particular point. As firearms became more lethal at greater ranges beginning in the mid-19th century, defensive fortifications grew in importance. Defenses became so strong, it took increasingly greater firepower and mass to break through them.[30] Consequently, commanders were warned not to piecemeal or disperse their forces: attempting to be strong everywhere meant they would be strong nowhere. Mass dominated land warfare, and planners focused on how to improve means of transportation and communication to ensure mass was available at the right place, at the right time, before the enemy was aware of it. F. W. Lanchester's "N-squared law," which postulated that as quantitative superiority increased for one side, its loss rate correspondingly decreased by the square root, lent a modicum of scientific credence to this belief in mass.[31]

This principle also seemed to hold true for air war. Early operations of the Eighth Air Force in World War II had only slight impact on the German war machine while also suffering high loss rates. General Ira Eaker, the Eighth's commander, argued this was because his forces were not large enough. In order to ensure a target could be effectively struck, while at the same time providing defensive protection, bomber formations had to include at least three hundred aircraft.[32] That figure proved low. German defenses were so formidable before the arrival of American escort planes that it took extremely large formations to ensure low casualty rates for the bombers—Lanchester's "law" seemingly proved in practice. Moreover, bombing accuracy was far less than expected, due partly to German defenses and deception and partly to abysmal weather. As a consequence, to destroy a target the size of a small house, a force of 4,500 heavy bombers carrying a total of nine thousand tons of bombs was required.[33]

Unfortunately, this process took time to neutralize a major system within a country. Hundreds of bombers were required to take down a single oil refinery, but then the strike force would have to move to another target on the next mission. Because there were hundreds of targets to be struck, each requiring a massive strike, the Germans were able to rebuild their facilities between attacks. In other words, the absence of precision forced air power into a battle of attrition that relied on accumulative effects, essentially driving it down to the tactical level. An outstanding example of this in World War II concerns the German oil refinery at Leuna. This important facility had extremely powerful anti-aircraft gun defenses as well as smoke generating machines to hide the refinery from Allied bombardiers. As a consequence, only 2.2 percent of all bombs dropped on Leuna actually impacted in the refinery's production area. Leuna therefore had to be struck twenty-two times during the last year of the war to put it out of commission. As the US Strategic Bombing Survey concluded, it would have been far more effective to drop a few bombs accurately than to "string 500-lb. bombs over the whole target."[34] Exactly true.

The numbers regarding bomb accuracy changed over time. The Vietnam War saw the first extensive use of precision guided munitions (PGM) during the Linebacker campaigns of 1972, and this allowed American aircraft to demolish that proverbial "small house" with only 190 tons of bombs carried by 95 aircraft.[35] Desert Storm introduced an improvement in accuracy, combined with stealth technology, that allowed a remarkably low loss rate per sortie (less than .05 percent). Aircraft could thus safely hit more targets in a given time period—parallel operations were possible. Few will forget the cockpit videos of laser-guided bombs flying down air vents and into bunker doorways. Only a small percentage of the total tonnage dropped was precision guided, and even they sometimes missed their targets; nonetheless, when using PGM and in suitable weather, our house now only needed one bomb and a single aircraft.[36] This combination of accuracy and stealth meant that targets were struck and neutralized quickly and safely.

The result of the trend towards "airshaft accuracy" in air war is a denigration in the importance of mass. PGM provide density, mass per unit volume, which is a more efficient measurement of force. In short, targets are no longer massive, and neither are the aerial weapons used to neutralize them.[37] One could argue that all targets are precision targets—even individual tanks, artillery pieces or infantrymen. There is no logical reason why bullets or bombs should be wasted on empty air or dirt. Ideally, every shot fired should find its mark.[38] If this sort of accuracy and continued stealth protection are attainable on a routine basis, the political, economic and logistics implications are great. Objectives can be threatened, and if necessary attacked, with little collateral damage or civilian casualties, at low cost and low risk since few aircraft will be required. It will also require a vastly reduced supply tail: only a handful of cargo aircraft would have been necessary to supply all the PGM needed each day during the Gulf War. This may present air commanders with an unusual problem.

Because precision is possible, it will be expected. Air warfare has thus become highly politicized. Air commanders must be extremely careful to minimize civilian casualties and collateral damage. All bombs are becoming political bombs, and air commanders must be aware of this emerging constraint. For example, as a result of U.S. strikes against Iraq during June 1993 in retaliation for an attempted assassination of former president George Bush, some European sources expressed concern because the cruise missiles used were "less than totally reliable." Eight Iraqi civilians were reportedly killed in the thirty-missile strike, and this was considered by some as excessive.[39]

It is safe to assume the omnipresent eye of the CNN camera will be an integral part of any future military operation. Hundreds of millions of people worldwide will judge the appropriateness of everything an air commander does.[40] This reality must be factored into the decision process, because in the future airmen may be required to wage war bloodlessly and delicately. The research in the area of non-lethal weapons is certainly a response to this trend. Although the ideal of bloodless war, sought by military leaders for centuries, has proven to be elusive, the quest continues.[41] Air power, because of its intrinsically precise and discriminate nature—properties that are increasing—may finally produce that coveted grail. At the same time, the evolving world situation indicates that America will become more involved in operations short of war, such as peacekeeping missions or humanitarian relief. The airdrop of food to Muslims in Bosnia is an example of this trend. These "food bomb" operations may become increasingly prevalent as our leaders turn to more peaceful applications of air power to achieve political objectives.

8 ⟶

Air Power's unique characteristics necessitate that it be centrally controlled by airmen.

Air warfare cannot be separated into little packets; it knows no boundaries on land and sea other than those imposed by the radius of action of the aircraft; it is a unity and demands unity of command.

—Air Marshal Arthur Tedder

General Carl Spaatz once commented in exasperation that soldiers and sailors spoke solemnly about the years of experience that went into training a surface commander, thus making it impossible for outsiders to understand their arcane calling. Yet, they all felt capable of running an air force. That comment, echoed by American airmen for decades, was at the root of their calls for a separate air force.

Many early air theorists believed air power would never be able to grow and reach its true potential if it was dominated by surface officers. Air power was so unlike traditional warfare, officers raised in the army and navy would have difficulty understanding it. (Obviously, the task was not insurmountable; virtually all the early airmen began their careers as soldiers and sailors.) On a more practical level, the question of who controlled air power became an administrative one. If the air force was subservient to the other services, then it was those services that determined such things as organization, doctrine, force structure and manning. The American Army Air Service, for example, was commanded by non-aviators, divided up and attached to individual surface units, was told what types of aircraft to procure and what missions to fly with those aircraft, and informed by non-flyers which airmen would be promoted and which would not. To say that airmen believed such a setup stifled their potential would be an understatement. For fundamental bureaucratic reasons airmen wanted a separate service. At a higher level of abstraction, they also believed that air power was most effective when commanded by an airmen who understood its unique characteristics.

Surface warfare is largely a linear affair defined by terrain and figures on a map. Although the modern battlespace has expanded dramatically, ground forces still have a primarily tactical focus and tend to be concerned primarily with an enemy or obstacles to their immediate front. Certainly, ground commanders worry about events beyond their immediate reach, but when operations move at an average of a few miles each day, such concerns are long term. New weapons have extended the range armies can strike, and subsequently expanded their area of concern; nonetheless, this extension is slight relative to air power. An airplane can deliver several tons of ordnance in a few minutes at a distance of hundreds of miles, and this requires an ability to think in operational and strategic level terms. Airmen must take a broader view of war because the weapons they command have effects at broader levels of war. Space-based assets, as well as airborne systems such as AWACS and JSTARS, help provide a theater-wide perspective. Moreover, Desert Storm was truly a global air war—the first of its kind—with personnel all over the world playing direct roles. For example, space operators in Cheyenne Mountain, Colorado, detected and tracked Iraqi Scud launches and then relayed that information to Patriot batteries in Saudi Arabia. Similarly, B–52s launched from air bases in Louisiana flew non-stop to bomb targets in Iraq. Finally, airlifters flew dozens of missions each day from the United States to the Middle East to deliver supplies and personnel.

Airmen fear that if surface commanders controlled air power they would divide it to support their own operations to the detriment of the overall theater campaign. However, in a typical campaign operations ebb and flow; at times one sector is heavily engaged or maneuvering, while at other times it is static and quiescent—and this status is often determined by the enemy. As a result, if air power is parceled out it may be sitting idle in one location while flying continuously in another. Although this is also true of ground units, they generally have only a limited ability to assist their comrades on another part of the front. Air power can quickly intervene over an entire theater, regardless of whether it is used for strategic or tactical purposes. To mete it out to different surface commanders would make it virtually impossible to shift air power, rapidly and efficiently, from one area in the theater to another to maximize its effectiveness.

To airmen, the necessity of centralized control has been amply demonstrated. Since World War I there has been an inexorable move towards greater centralized control of air power as aircraft have achieved greater range and firepower. Initially, all air forces were controlled by tactical surface commanders; today, virtually all of the world's air forces are independent. This trend has been illustrated in several examples. In the

North African campaign of 1942 the RAF was divided into packages and controlled by ground commanders. The results were disastrous and led to fundamental doctrinal changes.[42] On the other hand, the air campaigns of General George Kenney in the Southwest Pacific and those of Hoyt Vandenberg in Europe demonstrated an extremely effective use of air assets at the theater level. Korea was another negative example, with Air Force and Navy air assets fighting separate wars with little coordination. Vietnam saw this situation repeated—although the Air Force itself violated the principle of central control of air assets. Due to struggles within the service, Seventh Air Force in South Vietnam fought the air war in-country, Thirteenth Air Force directed air operations in Thailand, and Strategic Air Command fought yet another campaign with its B–52 strikes.

In Desert Storm things finally came together. A Joint Force Air Component Commander (JFACC) was appointed, General Charles Horner, to control all fixed-wing assets in theater, including those of other coalition countries. The synergies gained from diverse air forces working together as a team with one commander to focus their efforts played a major role in victory. During this combat test the JFACC concept worked, and will therefore be the organizational option of choice in the future. This is especially important because future conflicts may not have the overwhelming air assets available that were present in Desert Storm. In such instances tough decisions regarding prioritization will have to be made by those who understand air power.

9 ⟶

Technology and air power are integrally and synergistically related.

Science is in the saddle. Science is the dictator, whether we like it or not. Science runs ahead of both politics and military affairs. Science evolves new conditions to which institutions must be adapted. Let us keep our science dry.

—General Carl M. Spaatz

A recent U.S. Army pamphlet states that man, not technology, has always been and will always be the dominant force in war: "War is a matter of heart and will first; weaponry and technology second."[43] The centrality of the infantryman and his rifle is a recurring theme in the Army's culture. This vision depreciates the importance of technology, and is therefore not subscribed to by most airmen.

Air power is the result of technology. Man has been able to fight with his hands or simple implements and sail on water using wind or muscle power for millennia, but flight required advanced technology. As a consequence of this immutable fact, air power has enjoyed a synergistic relationship with technology not common to surface forces, and this is part of the airman's culture.[44] Air power depends upon the most advanced developments in aerodynamics, electronics, metallurgy, and computer technology. When one considers the space aspects of air power this reliance on technology becomes even more obvious. One has only to look at how land warfare has advanced this century; the evolution of machine guns, tanks and artillery has proceeded at a fairly steady pace. Certainly that pace has been more rapid than in any past comparable time period, but it pales in comparison to the advance in air power from Kitty Hawk to the space shuttle.

More importantly, the United States has achieved a formidable dominance in this area. Americans have a tendency to adopt technological solutions to problems, and this is evidenced in our approach to war.[45] Consequently, we have developed the most technologically advanced military in the world. With some exceptions our equipment, in all branches, is unmatched. Indeed, in some areas our dominance is so profound few countries even choose to compete with us, and this superiority is especially true in air power. Iraq simply refused the challenge; it seldom rose to contest with coalition fighters, and after two weeks its planes began fleeing to Iran to escape destruction. Similarly, only the former Soviet Union was able to approach us in the size of strategic airlift and inflight refueling forces, and those capabilities have rapidly atrophied after the empire's dissolution. The size and sophistication of American air power relative to the rest of the world is, at present, staggering. A recent RAND study found that the U.S. has more F–15s in its inventory than the rest of the world (excluding our allies and the former Soviet Union) has front-line combat aircraft combined. Considering that air forces require a level of technology and economic investment that only the richest or most advanced nations can afford, this favorable balance can be expected to continue.[46] Finally, none can duplicate American space infrastructure that has so revolutionized reconnaissance, surveillance and communications functions. Today, only the United States can project power globally, and that is a fact of enormous significance.

There will always be surprises, but it is not likely this technological edge will significantly change over the next few decades. Although the U.S. defense budget is severely shrinking in the aftermath of the Cold War, that of Russia has been slashed far more, totaling barely one-sixth that of the U.S.[47] Similarly, when considering the aeronautical R&D base, the United States has more than twice as many wind tunnels, jet and rocket engine test facilities, space chambers, and ballistic ranges than the rest of the world combined, while at the same time maintaining a qualitative edge. Of note, however, this superiority is shrinking as countries in Europe and Asia are accelerating their own aerospace industries: complacency is not appropriate.[48]

It has been argued that warfare is presently experiencing a military-technical revolution (MTR), and that this is the third such MTR in history; the first two being the invention of gunpowder and then the explosion of the late nineteenth and early twentieth centuries resulting in the railroad, machine gun, aircraft and submarine. John Warden goes farther, acknowledging the existence of the present MTR, but arguing it is actually the first such event.[49] He maintains the current leap in technology is so profound it makes prior changes appear as minor evolutionary steps. Regardless of whether this is the first or third MTR, air power is most affected because advancing technologies in space, computers, electronics, low observable weapons and information systems will enhance those services that rely on technology to decide the issue of war.

10 ➜

Air Power includes not only military assets, but an aerospace industry and commercial aviation.

> *With us air people, the future of our nation is indissolubly bound up in the development of air power.*
>
> **—General Billy Mitchell**

A collection of airplanes does not equal air power, and almost all theorists have realized this. As early as 1921 Mitchell wrote about the importance of a strong civil aviation industry, the role of government in building that industry, and of the importance of instilling an "airmindedness" in the people.[50] His later writings made these points even more emphatically. Similar sentiments were echoed by Alexander Seversky and most recently by air leaders who spoke of the United States—the inventor of the airplane—as an "aerospace nation."[51] The vast size of the United States and the need to connect the east and west coasts, and indeed Alaska and Hawaii, demanded a rapid, reliable and cost-effective method of transportation. The development of various airline companies—still the largest and most financially powerful in the world—were a direct result of American geography and the need it engendered.

Recognizing such economic and cultural imperatives, men like Mitchell and Seversky stressed that air power was far more than just airplanes. As discussed above, the technology required to develop first-rate military aircraft was so enormous, complex and expensive, it was essential that government and business play active roles. In the early years this equated to government subsidy of airports, airway structures, location beacons, weather stations, and support for research and development. The investment required for this new industrial field was simply too great for businesses to handle on their own. It was also assumed that military and commercial aircraft would have similar characteristics and thus would enjoy a symbiotic design relationship. Douhet and Seversky for example noted it was quite feasible to convert civilian airliners into military bombers or cargo aircraft.[52] More importantly, the skills needed to build, maintain and pilot these aircraft were also similar. Theorists saw a close relationship developing in aviation that would produce a pool of trained personnel who passed back and forth between the military and civilian sectors—mechanics, pilots, navigators, air traffic controllers, etc. In essence, there was an interdependence between the two sectors that was not present in armies or even navies. The capability of an armored force, for example, did not rely on the automobile industry or the teamsters union to the same degree an air force was dependent on the aircraft industry and airline pilots associations. More importantly, the quality of this aerospace complex is crucial. If transportation is indeed the essence of civilization, then aviation is the one industry in which America must remain dominant. The United States has often been in the forefront of emerging technologies—railroads, shipbuilding, automobiles, electronics and computers—only to later retreat from the field, leaving it to competitors. She cannot afford to do that in the air and space. Although the current status is favorable, negative trends must be avoided.

Aerospace industry sales topped $140 billion in 1991. The world's airlines overwhelmingly fly American airframes. Although the European Airbus has been able to maintain a world market share of about 15–20 percent in the large commercial jet category, the remaining 80 percent belongs to Boeing and Douglas. Moreover, the new Boeing 777, although not yet having flown, has already garnered nearly 150 orders from airlines worldwide—coincidentally, 80 percent of the market.[53] Internally, this means the aerospace industry has a percentage value of the U.S. gross national product behind only agriculture and automobiles. This has led to a trade surplus of over $30 billion in 1991, ahead of the traditional leader, agriculture, by a wide margin. At the same time, the number of air passengers continues to rise, as does the value and weight of air cargo. In addition, approximately one million people are employed in the American aerospace industry, making it the tenth largest in the country.[54] All this comes at a time when railroads are in decline, and our commercial ship building industry has all but disappeared. These figures translate into an extremely powerful and lucrative aerospace industry dominated by the United States. As already noted, the superiority of American military air and space assets is even more profound than in the commercial sector. No country in the world can rival us in the size, capability, diversity and quality of our air and space forces.[55] Unfortunately, this dominance may be in danger as a result of massive downsizing after our victory in the Cold War. One source states that the U.S. is falling behind Europe and Japan in the race to maintain primacy in satellite communications. It is therefore important to remember that American dominance in air and space is not automatic but must be constantly reasserted.[56]

Finally, the theorists urged that Americans think of themselves as an air power nation in the way generations of Englishmen had considered themselves a maritime nation. They must see their destiny in the air and in the space. To a great degree this may already be true. It is perhaps not just the allure of the special effects that has made movies like "Star Trek," "Star Wars," "The Right Stuff," "Top Gun" and others of that genre so popular in America.[57] In a very real sense, air power is a state of mind.

*   *   *

These then are my Ten Propositions Regarding Air Power. Most have an "ancient" pedigree: Douhet, Mitchell, Trenchard and others from aviation's earliest years understood and articulated them. Others were mere prophecies and needed a trial in war to determine their veracity. In some cases, such as number four regarding the link between targeting and intelligence and number eight dealing with centralized control, they had to be tried and tested in several wars before they were understood. Other propositions, such as number seven regarding the importance of precision, are just beginning to show their significance, and await future conflicts to prove their correctness beyond doubt.

Nonetheless, these propositions in their totality show air power to be a revolutionary force that has transformed war in less than a century. The fundamental nature of war—how it is fought, where it is fought, and by whom it is fought—has been altered. It is an unfortunate characteristic of air theorists that they long promised more than their chosen instrument could deliver. Theory outran technology, and airmen too often were in the untenable position of trying to schedule inventions to fulfill their predictions.[58] It appears those days are now past. Air power has passed through its childhood and adolescence, and the wars of the past decade, especially in the Persian Gulf, have shown it has now reached maturity.

On the Ten
Propositions. . .

About six years ago when Air Force Manual 1–1, *Basic Aerospace Doctrine of the U.S. Air Force*, was being re-written, then-Lt Gen. Michael Dugan, the Deputy Chief of Staff for Plans and Operations, proposed an unusual idea. Doctrine manuals were fine, but he wanted something brief and succinct, something that encapsulated the essence of air power. His ultimate goal: to produce a list of principles or rules of air power so succinct they would fit on a wallet-size card that airmen could carry in their pocket. My first reaction was one of skepticism. As a historian I had been taught to eschew simple solutions, formulas, models, and similar gimmicks that attempted to deal with complex problems. Yet, as one observer phrased it: "The consistency of the principles of war indicates that despite the doubts expressed by military theoreticians concerning their validity, they satisfy a deep need in military thinking."[59] These "needs" are a psychological search for guidelines when in chaos, the tendency to apply scientific concepts of cause and effect to daily activities, and the desire for an understandable belief system to use as an educational tool for young officers.

The general's proposal faded, but in truth, it never left my mind. The more I thought about it, the more appealing it seemed. Truly good writing, in my view, should be short, swift, and to the point. As Mark Twain said: "If I'd had more time I would have written less." Capturing the essence of what airmen believe about air power and putting it into a concise, understandable, but not simplistic format, was a challenge.

A catalyst was introduced when I was preparing a course on the history of air power theory. Reading the works of the top theorists: Douhet, Trenchard, Mitchell, Slessor, the officers at the Air Corps Tactical School, Seversky, Warden, and others brought many similarities to light. Even though living in different times, different places and different circumstances, these men had distilled certain principles, rules, precepts and lessons that seemed timeless and overarching. Some of these had been demonstrated in war, others were mere predictions. After seventy-five years, however, I think there have been enough examples of air power employment and mis-employment to derive some propositions—"principles" would be too grand a term—from the theories. First, however, let me briefly describe some of air power's unique characteristics—some strengths and some weaknesses—from which these propositions derive.

Even before the airplane was invented writers sensed that the medium of the air possessed intrinsic qualities that could be exploited for war, and it is quite amazing how quickly after the Wright Brothers first flew in 1903 that military men were positing its use as a weapon. During the 1911 war between Italy and Turkey in Libya, airplanes were used for the first time in combat. Virtually all of the traditional air missions were employed: observation, air defense, air superiority, transport, ground attack, even bombing.[60] The world war that erupted a few years later saw all these air missions refined. By the end of the Great War there was general agreement, among both air and surface officers, regarding the unique strengths and weaknesses of airplanes.

Air power's attributes include range—even the flimsy planes of 1918 could fly several hundred miles; speed—over one hundred miles per hour; elevation—the ability to fly over hills, rivers, and forests that would serve as obstacles to surface forces; lethality—concentrated firepower could be directed at specific points on and behind the battle area; and flexibility, a combination of the other attributes that allowed airplanes to be used in many ways, in many different places, quickly. The limitations of air power were also apparent early on: gravity—unlike surface forces, airplanes could not live in their medium and had to land in order to refuel and rearm. This in turn meant aircraft were ephemeral—air strikes lasted but a few minutes and therefore lacked persistence. Although airplanes could indeed fly over obstacles, they were limited by bad weather and the night. In addition, just like surface forces, political restrictions could determine where aircraft flew, when, and for what purpose. Finally, aircraft could not occupy or hold ground. Even seventy-five years later these attributes and limitations generally hold true, although some have clearly been nibbled away at the edges.

It is significant to point out here that these various characteristics, positive and negative, have been used by both air and surface proponents over the years to justify their own views on how aircraft should be used in war. Airmen magnified the importance of the attributes while minimizing the limitations. Their goal was a separate service not subordinate to surface commanders. For their part, ground and sea advocates noted the limitations inherent in airplanes, while downplaying the positive aspects. Their intent was to maintain dominance of the new air arm. This political debate over whether air power was revolutionary or evolutionary, and whether therefore it should or should not be a separate service, occupied decades of heated argument and caused needless animosity. Today, all major countries have an air force as a separate service. More importantly, however, there is an awareness that separateness does not equal singularity. Wars are fought in many ways with many weapons. Seldom is one service used to wage a campaign or war, although one service may be dominant in them. The nature of the enemy and the war, the objectives to be achieved, and the price willing to be paid by the people will determine what military instruments will be employed and in what proportion. My purpose in this essay is to list and discuss what I see as propositions regarding air power in the hope that it will better inform those who employ military power to achieve the objectives established by the country's leaders.

Notes

1. Giulio Douhet, "Command of the Air," in *Command of the Air* (Washington: Office of Air Force History, 1983), 25. This is a reprint of the Dino Ferrari translation originally published in 1942.

2. Col John A. Warden III, *The Air Campaign* (NY: Pergamon-Brassey's, 1989), 10. He later implies this may not necessarily be true in low intensity conflict.

3. This does not apply of course to the new threat of ballistic missiles. Iraqi Scuds were a major menace in the Gulf War, and this threat will no doubt continue to grow in the years ahead.

4. The classic work on the evolution of the aircraft carrier and naval air doctrine is Clark G. Reynolds, *The Fast Carriers: Forging an Air Navy* (NY: McGraw-Hill, 1968).

5. Martin Blumenson, "A Deaf Ear to Clausewitz: Allied Operational Objectives in World War II," *Parameters* 23 (Summer 1993), 16. Napoleon commented that European generals saw too many things; whereas, he saw only one thing, the enemy army.

6. For a grimly pessimistic view regarding the inherently indecisive nature of land warfare, in any age, see Russell Weigley, *The Age of Battles: The*

Quest for Decisive Warfare from Breitenfeld to Waterloo (Bloomington: Indiana Univ Press, 1991).

7. Mancur Olson, Jr., in *The Economics of the Wartime Shortage* (Durham: Duke Univ Press, 1963), argues that Napoleonic and later German attempts in two world wars to starve Britain into submission were failures and never came close to success. On the other hand, naval embargoes can cause great hardship if imposed for a long period of time, as against Iraq since August 1990. Youssef M. Ibrahim, "Iraq is Near Economic Ruin but Hussein Appears Secure," *New York Times*, 25 Oct 1994, 1.

8. For the air power advocates, see Adm U. S. G. Sharp, *Strategy For Defeat: Vietnam in Retrospect* (San Rafael: Presidio, 1978) and Gen William Momyer, *Airpower in Three Wars* (Washington: GPO, 1978). For the opposing view, see Maj Mark Clodfelter, *The Limits of Air Power* (NY: Free Press, 1989).

9. Roger T. Ames, trans., *Sun-Tzu: The Art of Warfare* (NY: Ballantine, 1993), 115.

10. A typical example used by early airmen was the London air defenses of 1918 that included over six hundred aircraft to counter a German bomber force of approximately forty planes. Sqdn Ldr J. C. Slessor, "The Development of the Royal Air Force," *RUSI Journal* 76 (May 1931), 328.

11. This is an interesting instance where air power's unique strength is also a weakness: aircraft generally "get through" because aircraft on the defensive lack "stopping power." Precisely because a

ground defender can dig in and hold his position he can repel an attack; aircraft cannot.

12. The Battle of Britain remains the major notable exception. Partial victories for the defense might include the retreat to night operations by Royal Air Force (RAF) Bomber Command to escape German defenses, and the temporary lull in American bombing operations in fall 1943 after severe losses in daylight strikes.

13. The most notable exception to this principle was during the Battle of Britain when the RAF withheld a large portion of its forces from the air battle. However, this was done not for the traditional reasons for reserve employment, to exploit or to plug, but to husband scarce resources of men and planes. Had the RAF been equal to the Luftwaffe in numbers and possessed a ready supply of reinforcements, they would have gained little by holding back their forces. For a contrary view on the desirability of an air reserve see Warden, *The Air Campaign*, 115–27.

14. It may be as one airman put it, an air reserve should be considered while the battle for air superiority is still raging; once air superiority is achieved the need for a reserve loses its rationale. Gp Capt Gary Waters, RAAF, ltr to the author, 26 Jul 1993.

15. Douhet, 50.

16. Maj Gen Don Wilson, "Origins of a Theory of Air Strategy," *Aerospace Historian* 18 (Spring 1971), 19–25.

17. Slessor should not be taken out of context. *Air Power and Armies* was a collection of lectures he

had presented while an instructor at the British Army Staff College in the early 1930s. Given his audience, he was forced to address air power in the context of a land campaign. Nevertheless, he reminded his readers that the primary role of air power was to conduct strategic bombing operations against an enemy's centers of gravity. Wing Cmdr John C. Slessor, *Air Power and Armies* (London: Oxford Univ Press, 1936), 3.

18. Col John A. Warden III, "Air Power in the Twenty-First Century," in Richard H. Shultz, Jr. and Robert L. Pfaltzgraff, Jr., eds., *The Future of Air Power in the Aftermath of the Gulf War* (Maxwell AFB: Air Univ Press, 1992), 65.

19. Brig Gen William L. Mitchell, *Our Air Force: The Keystone of National Defense* (NY: Dutton, 1921), 15.

20. Interestingly, not only have most air theorists had a single, key target theory, but they have also been surprisingly prescriptive: *their* target is the key in all types of wars, in all types of situations and against all types of opponents.

21. David Albright and Mark Hibbs, "Iraq's Bomb: Blueprints and Artifacts," *Bulletin of the Atomic Scientists*, Jan/Feb 1992, 30–40.

22. For an overview of the origins of this subject, see Robert F. Futrell, "U.S. Army Air Forces Intelligence in the Second World War," in Horst Boog, ed., *The Conduct of the Air War in the Second World War* (NY: Berg, 1992), 527–52.

23. John Arquilla and David Ronfeldt, "Cyberwar is Coming!" *Comparative Strategy* 12 (Apr–Jun 1993), 143. This is an interesting article that argues "netwar" and "cyberwar"—the attack on a country's information and communications systems—will be the dominant feature of future wars.

24. This was an example I observed while working on the Air Staff in the Pentagon during the Gulf War. For an excellent critique of BDA in the Gulf War see Lt Col Kevin W. Smith, "Cockpit Video: A Low Cost BDA Source," CADRE paper, Air University, Maxwell AFB, AL, Dec 1993.

25. Gulf War Air Power Survey, Vol II: Effects and Effectiveness Report (Washington: Government Printing Office, 1993), 303.

26. This subject was suggested to me by a student at the School of Advanced Airpower Studies, Maj Jason Barlow. His seminal master's thesis, "Strategic Paralysis: An Airpower Theory for the Present," (1992) first raised my consciousness to the symbiotic relationship between centers of gravity and how best to impact that relationship.

27. Robert L. Helmhold, *Rates of Advance in Historical Land Operations* (Bethesda: U.S. Army Concepts and Analysis Agency, Jun 1990), 1–3, 4–9.

28. John Boyd has remained a somewhat legendary figure among a small coterie of American military officers. He has never published his theories, but relies instead on lengthy briefings that include dozens if not hundreds of slides. For a good discussion, see James G. Burton, *The Pentagon Wars: Reform-*

ers *Challenge the Old Guard* (Annapolis: Naval Institute Press, 1993).

29. For an excellent discussion see Col Dennis M. Drew, "Insurgency and Counterinsurgency: American Military Dilemmas and Doctrine," CADRE paper, Air University, Maxwell AFB, Ala, 1989, 39–40.

30. At the Third Battle of Ypres (1917), the preliminary British artillery bombardment consisted of 4,283,550 shells, costing $110,000,000, weighing 107,000 tons, and requiring 35,666 truckloads to transport them from the railhead to the battlefield. Maj Gen J. F. C. Fuller, *Machine Warfare* (Washington: Infantry Journal Press, 1943), 17.

31. F. W. Lanchester, *Aircraft in Warfare: The Dawn of the Fourth Arm* (London: Constable, 1916), 39–65.

32. James Parton, *"Air Force Spoken Here": General Ira Eaker and the Command of the Air* (NY: Adler & Adler, 1986), 290.

33. Gen Michael Dugan, "The Air War," *U.S. News & World Report*, 11 Feb 1991, 27.

34. US Strategic Bombing Survey, "Oil Division: Leuna," Report no. 115. Washington, 1946, 51.

35. Dugan, 27.

36. Ibid. Richard P. Hallion, *Storm Over Iraq: Air Power and the Gulf War* (Washington: Smithsonian, 1992), 303–07. The potential downside of this situation is that one terrorist with a satchel charge could not have eliminated 4,500 bombers.

37. It should also be noted that stealthy effects can also be generated by speed—such as in a ballistic missile with fifteen meter accuracy like the Soviet SS–21. Such missiles are of course limited by their expense and non-reusable nature.

38. An alternative view: the psychological effect of bombing is so devastating that even a miss can have a great impact. There is a story told of the Iraqi troop commander who when asked why he surrendered replied it was the B–52 strikes. When it was pointed out his division had never been attacked by B–52s, he responded that was true, but he had seen a division that had been hit by B–52s. Hallion, 218.

39. Francis Tusa and Glenn W. Goodman, Jr., "Who Benefits from Baghdad Bombing?" *Armed Forces Journal International*, Aug 1993, 10. It should also be noted there may be countermeasures to at least some types of precision weapons. Miniature jammers that reportedly can disrupt the signals of GPS guidance systems have been developed and could be easy to mass produce. John G. Ross, "A Pair of Achilles Heels," *Armed Forces Journal International*, Nov 1994, 21-23.

40. For an excellent discussion of this issue, see Lt Col Marc Felman, "The Military/Media Clash and the New Principle of War: Media Spin." Master's thesis, School of Advanced Airpower Studies, Air University, 1992. In addition, the U.S. Army's new doctrine manual emphasizes the importance of the media in shaping military operations. Department of the Army, FM 100–5, *Operations*, Jun 1993, 3–11.

41. Lt Col Alan W. Debban, "Disabling Systems: War-Fighting Options for the Future," *Airpower Journal* 7 (Spring 1993), 44–50; Mary C. Fitzgerald, "The Russian Image of Future War," *Comparative Strategy*, 13 (Summer 1994), 167–80. On the other hand, one study argues the American public has more often called for stern action against an enemy when casualties mount. Thus, an enemy who tries to shed American blood in the hope it will break public will has generally provoked the opposite response. Benjamin C. Schwarz, "The Influence of Public Opinion Regarding Casualties on American Military Intervention: Implications for U.S. Regional Deterrence Strategies." RAND draft paper, Santa Monica, Calif, 1993.

42. Vincent Orange, *Coningham* (Washington: Center for Air Force History, 1992), 132–37.

43. Gen Gordon R. Sullivan and Lt Col James M. Dubik, "Land Warfare in the 21st Century," Strategic Studies Institute paper, Carlisle Barracks, Pa, Feb 1993, 27.

44. To illustrate, when one visits an air museum the emphasis is on aircraft and weaponry displays; at an army museum the focus is on people, uniforms and personal armament and equipment. For an excellent discussion of these cultural differences, see Carl H. Builder, *The Masks of War: American Military Styles in Strategy and Analysis* (Baltimore: Johns Hopkins, 1989).

45. Russell Weigley, *The American Way of War* (NY: Macmillan, 1973) advances this thesis most strongly.

46. Christopher J. Bowie, et al, "Trends in the Global Balance of Airpower," RAND Study, Santa Monica, Calif, Jun 1993, 2, 49. This is especially compelling when it is noted the F–15 is 95–0 in air-to-air combat engagements.

47. In 1992 the U.S. defense budget was $242.7 billion; Russia's total that year was $39.6 billion. Other major countries and their defense budgets in 1992: China—$22.3b, France—$21.8b, UK—$20.7b, Germany—$19.2b, Japan—$16.9b, Saudi Arabia—$14.5b, Italy—$10.6b and Kuwait—$10.1b. (All figures are given in 1985 dollars and using IMF exchange rates.) International Institute for Strategic Studies, *The Military Balance, 1993–1994* (London: Brassey's, 1993), 224–28.

48. "An Aerospace Challenge and the Path Toward a New Horizon," Arnold Engineering Development Center paper and briefing, Jun 1993.

49. Col Andy Krepinevich, "The Military-Technical Revolution," unpublished OSD paper, Aug 1992. Warden's position is found in a letter to Paul Wolfowitz, no date but early Sep 1992, commenting on the Krepinevich study.

50. Mitchell, *Our Air Force*, 143–58, 199–216.

51. Alexander P. de Seversky, *Victory Through Air Power* (NY: Simon & Schuster, 1942), 329; Donald B. Rice, "Global Reach/Global Power," Air Force White Paper, Dec 1992, 15.

52. Douhet, 124; Seversky, 296.

53. Harvey Elliot, "America Takes Over the Skies," *London Times*, 10 Jan 94, 21.

54. All of these statistics come from James W. Chung, "Whither the U.S. Aerospace Industry?" *Breakthroughs*, Winter 1992/93, 12–18.

55. The emerging dominance of air power within American military strategy is covered in Col Dennis M. Drew, "We Are An Aerospace Nation," *Air Force*, Nov 1990, 32–36.

56. "Panel Says U.S. Losing Race for Next Generation Satellite Communications," *Aerospace Daily*, 30 Jul 1993, 168–69. For a good discussion, see Maj Steven Wright, "Aerospace Strategy for the Aerospace Nation." Master's thesis, School of Advanced Airpower Studies, Air University, 1993.

57. For an excellent overview of the connection between aviation and American culture, see Robert Wohl, "Republic of the Air," *Wilson Quarterly* 17 (Spring 1993), 107–17.

58. Of great interest, this has been precisely the opposite regarding military space operations, where the technology has far out paced any coherent doctrine on how to employ space systems effectively.

59. Svi Lanir, "The Principles of War and Military Thinking," *Journal of Strategic Studies* 16 (Mar 1993), 1–17.

60. Renato D'Orlando, trans., *The Origin of Air Warfare*, 2nd ed. (Rome: Historical Office of the Italian Air Force, 1961).

Suggested Readings

Gen. Henry H. Arnold. *Global Mission.* New York: Harper & Bros, 1949.

Richard G. Davis. *Carl A. Spaatz and the Air War in Europe.* Washington: Center for Air Force History, 1994.

Alexander de Seversky. *Victory through Air Power.* New York: Simon and Schuster, 1942.

Giulio Douhet. *Command of the Air.* Washington: Office of Air Force History, 1983.

Robert F. Futrell. *Ideas, Concepts, and Doctrine: A History of Basic Thinking in the United States Air Force, 1907–1964.* Maxwell AFB: Air University, 1974.

Richard P. Hallion. *Storm Over Iraq: Air Power and the Gulf War.* Washington: Smithsonian, 1992.

Strike from the Sky: The History of Battle field Attack. 1911–1945. Washington: Smithsonian, 1989.

I. B. Holley. *Ideas and Weapons.* Washing-